YAHWEH'S
OTHER
SHOE

Kilian McDonnell, O.S.B.

Editor: Martha Meek
Cover design: David Manahan, o.s.b. Photos by
iStockphoto.com and Oleg Prikhodko.
Typographer: Thom Tammaro

"Eve and the Hermeneutic Task," "Kilian Parks Car
C," and "Joseph, I'm Pregnant by the Holy Ghost"
appeared in *The National Catholic Reporter;* "A Place
to Hide: Light Off" and "A Place to Hide: Light On,"
in slightly different versions, appeared in *Weavings.*

Library of Congress Cataloging-in-Publication Data

McDonnell, Kilian.
    Yahweh's other shoe / Kilian McDonnell.
        p.   cm.
    ISBN-13: 978-0-9740992-2-4
    ISBN-10: 0-9740992-2-8
    1. Christian poetry, American.   I. Title.

PS3613.C3878Y34   2006
811'.6—dc22
                                                2006017891

I dedicate this book
to Martha Meek, Jay Meek,
and Anna George Meek,
a family of prize-winning poets,

who witness
to the enduring place of poetry
in the nation's
substantive life.

CONTENTS

Ars scribendi / Ars moriendi   1

WE WALK WITH SARAH

Eve and the Hermeneutic Task   4
Yahweh's Other Shoe   6
God Cheats   8
Deborah, Lady Jael, and the Tent Peg   10
Sarah Giggles Behind the Tent   13
Isaiah Sees Wonder within the Walls of the World   14

DRINKING A NEW KIND OF WATER

Joseph, I'm Pregnant by the Holy Ghost   18
Something for the Census   20
Catching Fish from Shore   22
The Ignorant Mary at Cana   24
A New Kind of Water at Jacob's Well   27
Peter's Wife   30
The One Called Judas   32

THE FATHER EMPTIES HIS COFFERS

The Ox's Broad Behind   36
Hogs and Salvation   38
Rolling the Stone from the Grave   40
No One Loves Me   42
I Have Two Sons   44

THE FREIGHT OF THE WORLD

Dachau   48
Nelson Mandela   49
Srebrenica   50
Coming Home in Kosovo   52
The Day of the Cardboard Cutters   54
Elected Muscle at Monastic Matins   56

WHAT I SEE FROM THE BELL TOWER

In Praise of the Clay Angel   60
My Favorite Idol and the Other God   62
Lilacs and Galaxies   64
The Ladder Not Climbed, the Battle Not Fought   66
God Is Silent   68
John Berryman: *I Don't Think I Will Sing Any*
    More Just Now; or Ever   70
My Uncle Henry, the Lawyer   72
I've Come to See the Pope   74
A Place to Hide: Light Off   76
A Place to Hide: Light On   77
My First Hearing Aid   78

NOISES FROM THE CLOISTER

Lauds and Trouble   80

Saint John's Turkey Vultures   82

In Search of Fire   83

Thirst and Rot in the Monastery   84

Kilian Parks Car C   86

If I Reach Eighty-Six . . .   88

The Laying on of Hands   90

I'll Do It Tomorrow   92

The Death of Mount Saint Helena   94

French Verbs, Whiskey, Holiness   96

Sunday Morning   98

Notes on the Poems   101

PERSONAL ESSAY

A Poet in the Monastery:
  I Do Not Tell "Noble Lies"   104

ARS SCRIBENDI / ARS MORIENDI

*With apologies to Red Smith, Samuel Coleridge,
William Strunk, Jr., and E. B. White.*

Sit at a desk and open a vein.
Two grains of opium may bring you
to stately palaces in distant Xanadu,
but is it worth an addled brain?

Writing's a pain. Be short, be spare,
yourself will suffice, forswear to soar
(Mozart first played scales).
Bleed by the pails, cut the fat,

revise, polish like burnished lava.
Weep, bleed again, curb the breezy
me, dramatize, come not unhinged.
Dante walks out of hell unsinged.

WE WALK
WITH SARAH

EVE AND THE HERMENEUTIC TASK

*So when the woman saw that the tree was good for food
. . . she took of its fruit and ate; and she also gave some
to her husband. Genesis 3:6*

From the start she's ahead of him:
muscular of intellect,
confident in wit and face,
sensitive—but not circumspect,

so indifferent as gardener,
so tolerant of weeds. She scratches
abstractedly among the poppies, leans
against the tree in the middle of the patch.

But it's quite another matter
when it comes to laws of God and state.
She understands the hermeneutic task:
how to question, when to deprecate.

Not great on consultation.
Does not dither until her man
has spoken; alley-wise before
the alleys were part of city plans,

she listens to the serpent's doubts
about the meaning of God's word,
probes the tempter's hint about
the Maker's motives, so carefully blurred.

Quickly done. She bites,
hands the apple to her spouse,
standing quietly beside her.
Passive, he chews death upon his house.

Eve has the rib of equality and more:
the highest art and flame of God.
If Adam wags behind her like a pup,
he's free from blame? How very odd!

YAHWEH'S OTHER SHOE

*Abraham fell on his face and laughed, and said to
himself, "Can a child be born to a man who is
a hundred years old?" Genesis 17:17*

Really now, it's absurd. Funerals
    have been planned, plots selected,
        graves dug, the choir has practiced,
           lean nephews eager at the door.

At a hundred, palsied of hand,
    I should spurt my seed with vigor
        so the servants gathered at the well
           can jest of a legendary goat.

They point fingers at Sara, ninety,
    fruitful as a broken clay pot,
        now a pregnant grandmother,
           nine months gone, sleepless

nights while I snore loudly,
    backaches, a craving for Arabian
        figs not found in Mamre,
           waspish if the goat's milk

isn't fresh that morning. Sara lies
    at soup to your abrupt face.
        Oh, you keep your little promise,
           faithful to the last generation.

All this, I know, is symbolic
   of some vast cosmic intent,
      some system of opaque meanings
         about locating my story in your sovereignty.

Just so. I pasture my flocks in the valley
   where Persian Reeds and Lemon Grass
      grow lush and tall, waiting
         for your other shoe to fall.

GOD CHEATS

When the man saw that he did not prevail against Jacob,
he struck him on the hip socket; and Jacob's hip
was put out of joint as he wrestled with him. Genesis 32:25

Late we cross the ford of Jabbok;
wives, camels, sheep I send ahead.

Alone in the sanctuary of the night,
where only touch can see,

I wrestle with a stranger until dawn breaks,
sweat to sweat, flesh to mystery.

When I pin him, I'm stunned.
Not a stranger, but my God.

When Yahweh sees that I prevail,
He fouls me by a touch, unsocketing my hip.

I contended in the womb with hairy Esau
and won. I'm a mirror of my foes.

Yahweh pleads: *The day is near upon us,*
now let me go. But still I lock Him.

I held Esau's heel in the womb; I
do not surrender when I'm winning.

Not unless you bless me with a winner's blessing
that cannot be annulled. No sly cancellations.

In the failing mist I feel, then see His face.
Tell me your name, and I'll let you go.

The Almighty Con thrones upon the cherubim,
names me Israel, but not Himself.

With an extorted blessing, a new name,
I walk away limping.

DEBORAH, LADY JAEL, AND
THE TENT PEG

At that time Deborah, a prophetess, wife of
Lappidoth, was judging Israel. Judges 4:5

Iron's the new Lord.
Older kings cast
their crowns before it. But Israel
hugs its dull bronze.
To the new, triumph in battle.
To the old, untidy death.

Deborah, no scrubber of pots,
but war strategist, prophetess
to whom all Israel comes
for judgment, sits beneath
the palm tree between Ramah
and Bethel. Her man cooks stew.

From the shade she summons
General Barak to stand
before her, receive her word:
By a woman's hand will
Yahweh deliver into your
hands all Sisera's uncircumcised

kings with their nine-hundred
iron chariots, nine-hundred
apocalyptic steeds breathing
hot death like robber
gods unleashing fire
upon our antique bronze.

What need have we of iron
wheels when Yahweh is our
general, fights beside us?
Go, hide in the leafy trees
on the high slopes of Mount
Tabor to view the land below.

I myself will draw the iron
chariots and all the kings
and princes of Sisera to the plain.
You will see rank on rank
of chariots poised for charge.
At my sign, your foot soldiers

will descend like hornets from Gehenna.
When all the kings and chariots
are ranged in battle line
below Mount Tabor, Deborah
shouts *Charge*. The black cloud
swarms down the slope

to chariots mired in the mud
Yahweh had made for Sisera.
The warrior flees on foot
to Lady Jael, standing before
her tent tied to the terebinth tree.
She invites him to enter, offers

milk, bread, pillow,
covers him with a rug from Sidon.
Lady Jael drives a tent
peg through his head,
pins him to the ground.
And then he's dead.

Deborah shakes out her skirts,
returns to sit in the shade
of the palm tree between
Ramah and Bethel, giving
judgment to all Israel.
Lady Jael tidies up the tent.

SARAH GIGGLES BEHIND THE TENT

So Sarah laughed to herself, saying, "After I have grown old, and my husband is old, shall I have pleasure?" Genesis 18:12

My periods with cataracts of blood
have ceased these fifty years. I'm wrinkled.

Yet I'm to have pleasure like a bride.
It must be dry-well me. Imagine!

At ninety, shall my waters
break, rush down this unused slope?

When gods say silly things you laugh.
Even Abraham breaks up, falls on his face.

Behind the tent I titter at the word
of the Lord, then lie to Yahweh's face.

My belly grows heavy; I spread my legs
like other wives. Silly things

are true. The Lord has his lame jest.
Yahweh names our boy, *God laughs.*

ISAIAH SEES WONDER WITHIN THE WALLS OF THE WORLD

I, I am he who comforts you. Isaiah 51:12

I've got unclean lips, the people
grow fat hearts, but God
has shown something of his glory.

Elected Voice of God, I speak
comfort to Jerusalem, Mrs. Isaiah,
and all Israel these forty years.

Of the Lord, high and lifted up
I see the fringe only,
the hem of his holiness.

I hear only whispers of his breath,
echoes of distant liturgies.
No visions face to face,

no sight beyond the gate
of the temple court, but within
walls of this world I see

Eve, garlic, leeks,
cedars of Lebanon, leaping
deer and howling jackals

as shadows of splendor, traces
of the Shekinah over the temple.
The press of God's glory makes

the gate hinges groan,
while white boulders from Solomon's
quarries form one crippled choir.

DRINKING
A NEW KIND
OF WATER

JOSEPH, I'M PREGNANT
BY THE HOLY GHOST

Her husband Joseph, being a righteous man . . .
planned to dismiss her quietly. Matthew 1:19

Life was simple before that angel
pushed open the kitchen door,
announced light and trouble, as though
a foe had roiled the bottom of the well
and now the pail brings up only

murky water. I'm chosen for some
terrible grace beyond the well.
After short light long dark,
left to stumble through the Sinai

Desert. No manna to gather, no quail
to catch. Nothing. When I tell Joseph
I'm pregnant by the Holy Ghost,
he stares, ox-dumb in hurt. I've asked

him to believe that I, God's
Moses-girl, part seas, give
Torah. He turns, leaves
without a word. Why should my dearest

love believe? Yahweh's not fair.
Where's the voice of light? Where
the pillar of fire? My man drops
me cold, as though I were a concubine

dismissed without a drachma for cheating
on her master's blanket with that
swarthy Roman soldier from the barracks.
Joseph doesn't expose me; I will not

be stoned. My heart eats Yahweh's
cinders; I drink the last date wine
gone sour at the dregs.
God does nothing. But I carry life.

SOMETHING FOR THE CENSUS

In those days a decree went out from Emperor Augustus that all the world should be registered. Luke 2:1

At Caesar's command they come to be counted,
   she leaning backward on the donkey
      protecting her heaviness against no particular threat,
         while Joseph haggles with the keeper of the inn.

No bed unoccupied, even closets are full,
   but the cattle caves are empty, except
      for the absolute sovereignty of ox and sheep
        and the high dominion of the doves making
                    soft noises.

Before they step through the swinging gate
   to smell fresh dung, last week's urine,
      she begins to gasp, moan, as women do
        when the pain is on them.

In the gathered straw the child spreads her legs,
   pushes, persuades, compels the child to leave
      into the spacious hands of her man,
        who wipes the boy, beds him where the cattle feed.

The Emperor in the palace will be the last to hear.
   A band of drunken angels in glory robes,
      besotted by the news, stumbles down singing
        to the unwashed, unmoored, witless in the fields.

Ranks of seraphim are stupefied: *God has come*
   to you in flesh, so you can come to God in flesh.
      And the great reeling throng from the throne of
                                                    splendor
         fills the sky above the town with raucous adoration.

They say, *Against the hill, in the grotto,*
   the Savior of us all is born as common as a butcher's son.
      They swaddle the little Lord in Nazareth rummage,
         push aside the feeding cow to lay him in the straw.

This year the census log reads: a dodgy eastern trio
   mustered by an errant star, and three from Galilee.
      The baby had made a ruckus and disturbed the peace,
         but they left by the Calvary road for parts unknown.

CATCHING FISH FROM SHORE

He saw James, son of Zebedee, and his brother John,
who were in their boats mending their nets. Mark 1:19

After their long night fishing
you don't mess with fishermen

with empty boats, empty stomachs,
a thousand fathoms of defeat.

If you poke an angry fire,
stand back. It flares out

like a dragon's tail.
Beware of sleeping monsters.

Do not, I repeat, do not
scoop honey from the lion's

carcass while the beast is still alive.
No jests, no small talk.

Stride silently past the boat,
as by a hearse, as though

you had a goal ahead,
and the sandy road is long.

He stops. Unbelievable!
He's going to say something.

I see you have no fish.
Catastrophe. Couldn't be worse.

After this the brothers
lay down their nets, leave their

boats behind and follow him.
The one with the open mouth is Father.

THE IGNORANT MARY AT CANA

*When the wine gave out, the mother of Jesus said to him,
"They have no wine." John 2:3*

Neighbors say my sudden rabbi
will be there with his sudden friends
I've not met. I get news now by chance,
as though we'd quarreled and he'd slammed
the door on parting. With his brothers I walk
eight miles to Cana, talking
of what we know and don't know.
Something's hidden, some secret archeology.
After thirty years of awl and hammer
abruptly he's the prophet of the day,
with disciples to run before him, keep
the crowds at bay. If the mystery has some
large design, I'm ignorant. In this pit
I have no spade. Deeper I can't dig.

The hearth room is cluttered with raisin breads,
early figs from Lebanon, mutton shanks,
and waist-high water jars,
gossiping women dissecting the groom.
As I set my wine-gift upon the kitchen table
the aunts and nieces crowd me for facts
I don't have. I know nothing.
They tell me he's here with his disciples,
outside in the courtyard among the men

who strike the tambourines, pluck the lyre.
With the women from the kitchen I watch
my prophet/son arm over arm
with Peter, Judas, John, and friends
dancing a laughing circle around the bride
and groom, as though Yahweh decreed wedding
wine the first step toward the reign of God.
Kingdoms are also built with dance and drink.

In the kitchen—disaster.
We can see the bottom of the wine jugs
accusing like a curse from Deuteronomy.
Had Jesus and all his friends forgotten
their wine-gift, but toasted all the Jacobs
back to Adam, depleting the wine jugs,
bringing wedding wine-shame upon the house?
The mother of a prophet still has rights.
They have no wine, I tell him. *Woman,*
what concern is that to you or me?
My hour has not yet come.

I stagger from the two-edged sword
my son plunged firmly into my breast.
Bleeding rivers rise between us.
This is new. Yet in the bloody flow
the edge of mystery, unlike the unmanageable
edge of pain, is somewhat lifted.

This is not my kitchen. Nazareth is dead.
From forever, this is the Father's Cana.
Only he decrees the hour to rip
in two the curtain across the Holy of Holies.
His Father's eternal hour, like laws
of the Persians and the Medes, cannot be changed.
His son is not free. But by some unnamable
logic, I know my son will act.

I turn to the servants: *Do whatever he tells you.*
They pour in water, dip out wine.

I wonder: if a hundred and twenty
gallons is the measure of extravagance
at the beginning of glory,
what will be the end?

A NEW KIND OF WATER AT JACOB'S WELL

A Samaritan woman came to draw water, and Jesus said to her, "Give me a drink." John 4:7

Five husbands, a lover,
and six hundred wounds that never heal.
I pay dearly for each stolen night of dazzle,
each pilfered dawn.

Eternal passion usually lasts a year.
Then twelve long months including January—
a cold drunk: mean and smelly.
I move on, take my scars with me,
heirlooms pocked with holes from wars I've lost,
bitter seeds of bitter weeds that will bloom again.

Love's a romp.
With a swish of my skirt I can still snare a man.
Flat-chested, frog-faced women glare at me.
I've made off with six of theirs.

Near the synagogue I meet the pinched
rectitude of rabbis' scorn.
Mothers yank their children to the side
lest my shadow fall on them.

Other women go to Jacob's well
before the sun is high. Today I take my rope
and leather pail in the noonday heat.
As usual, no one there,
except this solitary Jew of thirty
sitting on the wall, watching.
Jewish snakes shed their skins in Samaria
on their way from temple piety in Jerusalem.
Too bad. Handsome, just my type.

No greeting. None expected.
I hear, *Give me a drink*.
Ill-mannered stranger, speaking to a woman
outside her house.
Am I a lumpy nobody?

He speaks of mystic water he can give,
a well within that flows forever.
Calls himself *I AM*.
The chill: he knows me.
Not just the trivial sand beneath my rug,
but my public pyramids.
Go, call your husband and come back.

I drop my pail, hurry into Sychar,
an apostle to my people.
The women say
any man who can count all the beds I've warmed
must be from God.
Oddly, they listen.

We hurry out to where Jacob watered his flocks.
For two whole days he stays with us,
pouring out a new kind of water.
I drink at his feet
kneeling beside the women of the town.

PETER'S WIFE

Do we not have the right to be accompanied by a believing wife, as do the other apostles and the brothers of the Lord and Cephas? 1 Corinthians 9:5

Charms still young, done with fishing
for today, he empties the pail of sardines,
which spill like silver shekels, small

bolts of lightning flooding from the money
changers sack when the Master
overturned the temple tables.

Peter stoops over our cracked basin
to wash his hands for supper; suddenly
tears in the water. The three denials,

like contaminated evidence, keep volunteering
at soup, in bed together. At dusk
he swore to die with him, blurting out

like some eager pubescent, a bumbling fire
yawing between quick boast
and quick bust, the rush of Jordan's

rapids, the water gone before
it comes. A wife knows these hidden
histories—only crocodile eyes

peering just above the murky water.
Not so smart in Godly wisdom,
but in bed I hear my apostolic

lover stir, thrash the covers, turn
once more. I know he's staring at the ceiling.
At dawn his pillow's wet again.

THE ONE CALLED JUDAS

Suddenly a crowd came, and the one called Judas,
one of the twelve, was leading them. He approached
Jesus to kiss him. Luke 22:47

Treason has its reasons mixed;
like love it's never pure.
Ask Peter. Trouble in the art
of loving is always at the door—
or halfway through, sure
to spill its treachery on the floor

for piety to see. Perfect
nudity, unscented, belongs
to the free: wild geese, or whales
in the sea. But I'm chained
to a man I love above
all men, who longs for a reign
above, some wispy plan.

Neither manic mumbling nor
sibyllic chatter. The man is sane,
wired to the will of his Father more
than any of us dare. Last week
he raised foul Lazarus, who'd lain
very dead. He's no frenzied freak.

In the years I've been with him
I've seen more miracles than Moses
saw. The master is a burning
bush still green, but his armies
are archangel mists. He won't
restore the Law and Kingdom.

A mystic loser, prophetic peril to
his people—and time for us to part,
for I've dressed the paschal Jew,
betrayer of our nation's hope.
They'll bind his wrists with rope.
But my treason has a tender heart.

THE FATHER
EMPTIES
HIS COFFERS

THE OX'S BROAD BEHIND

The younger of them said to his father, "Father, give me the share of the property that will belong to me." Luke 15:12

I'm nowhere, dying of rectitude.
I plow the same ruts each year
looking at the ox's broad behind.
My bunkered blood is stagnant.

> A knife cut me. I'll die
> a steer on the farm
> in manhood's ruins.

Falcon beak, vulture claw
pick at my crotch. No decadence for stadia.
I flute my buffo dreams. Where are
the girls? With mother at synagogue

> behind the grill, hearing
> precentors facing Ark
> chanting Torah toward Jerusalem.

Big brother lectures me once more
how to plow, how not to plow.
It never ends. I'll be buried
before the spigot's turned on.

I need the doubtful city,
back alleys, night noises,
unmade beds, the lumpy life

of disordered streets. I want space
to do my lion strut at water
holes in front of all the local prides.
Gangrene's creeping up my legs.

The old man's strong, may live
forever. I'm trapped. . . . I'll ask
him for my portion now.

HOGS AND SALVATION

So [the younger son] went and hired himself out
to one of the citizens of that country, who sent him
to his fields to feed the pigs. Luke 15:15

I'm strangely sober, my last shekel
gone on tavern girls and booze.
A Gentile in golden tasseled mantle
was looking for a boy to tend his piggery.

> Why not? Hunger is lean.
> Ask no Torah questions
> when the sty is your address.

When the short-legged devils roll
in foulest mud, you forget they're smart.
Sows drop fecal cookies on my feet,
hell's latrine. Stench clings like identity.

> No wonder the seven Maccabean
> brothers chose death to swallowing
> Greek pork. Wise men.

No boss-man lives beside this outhouse;
my castle of despair is downwind.
Will I starve in swill to my knees while
meat in my father's cupboard goes uneaten?

Why does an empty stomach
teach what Father's dumbest slave
knows after one day in his house?

The wide door stands always open,
the pantry shelves are never empty,
unprocurable wine from Spain in barrels.
The old man's been expecting company.

ROLLING THE STONE
FROM THE GRAVE

*But while he was still far off, the father saw him,
and was filled with compassion; he ran and put
his arms around him and kissed him.* Luke 15:20

Gone these three years
my youngest boy, all hunger on stilts,
varnisher of risk theory, refuses
to straddle, wounded by friendly spears.

     Eager for the strange streets.
     Did you ever hold a lion
     cub by the ear? Tell me.

Pulling weeds, worrying my cabbages,
I stop, turn to grab a hoe;
across the valley I see a speck
far off on the ascending road.

     There are specks and specks.
     I see them every day.
     Don't ask me why I stare.

Leaning on my hoe, I watch the speck
become a blob, the blob become
a man, the man become my son.
I run, trampling cabbages,

down the mountain road,
weeping, shouting idiocies,
laughing, arms gathering in.

I roll the stone from the grave. Losing
is loving with a leaky heart; finding
is the excess of the blood's expanding universe.
Buy Helbon wine. The cost be damned.

NO ONE LOVES ME

But when this son of yours came back, who has devoured your property with prostitutes, you killed the fatted calf for him! Luke 15:30

The Golden Nothing creeps home.
The kid who siphoned off your blood,
slit your purse, is back expecting
bows and offerings. You've crumbled with joy.

He trashes your new ox
cart, burns your barn,
comes purring back once more,

rubbing his adolescent fur against
your boney leg, waiting for your petting
hand. You wince, smile. The cycle
of eternal return. Your fault, only yours.

Tell me, just tell me why
this heedless, selfish cub
all claws and smiles, can

charm away the jagged slash upon
your face. The cut goes deeper than
the scar. No leash, no cage will do.
He scampers free to booze in back-

strip brothels. This son
of yours has the brass, cold
brass, to ask you for his portion

while you live. And now he's back,
hungry, broke, mauled by city cats,
leaving a trail of chaos and copulation,
licking self-inflicted wounds, scratching

at your front door to see
if he had left some loot
behind last time around.

Once more, the tattered plumage, polished
tears. You suggest I sing the kid
a Hallel psalm to celebrate his passing
over. But, I, too was trapped.

For years I bled fidelity
unsung. No new rags upon
my back. Am I an alley mongrel?

No, I will not join the joy.
I'm weary of forgiveness.
Let the lost stay lost.
Next month, he'll be gone.

I HAVE TWO SONS

His father came out and began to plead with him. Luke 15:28

Look, my older son. Come in.
I've two sons: I need them both.
One son is only half my life.
Without you I limp toward death.

> You smell the perfume of pink
> curtained brothels, and the reek
> of Gentile sties; but my nostrils

are hardened to the whiff of odors overripe,
his—and yours. Nothing new
in stenches' history. To me he smells
of the son who wears my best robe, the one

> your mother wove for me
> of twisted thread from Tyre.
> He smells of her and me.

And he was lost. Yes, you've slaved
for me these many years, as you remind
me now. All you see before you,
pastures, sheep, granaries, are yours.

> You're angry—Yes, I always
> take him back. You think
> I'm weak; he's the proof.

A lion cub snarls when I feed him,
pees only on my best rug,
tears up the Torah text, scratches
scabs on my face for blood; I purr.

> You think I give you
> pawed-over odds, tender
> debris he cast aside.

You say my love for him is a rogue wave,
smoothing sand but piling wreckage.
Love comes not from music of monotony,
sounding equal beats for every waltz and tango.

> The gold I give to him, I take
> from you? I'll run out of stash?
> No, I've hoards eyes don't see.

You count the coins too carefully.
Don't store my gold in spider holes.
You're my only son.
He's my only son.

THE FREIGHT
OF THE
WORLD

DACHAU

"Howl with the wolves," says the sign upon the wall.

Evil here has mass and density beyond tears,
the other side of rage.
In awe of unhinged venom and my complicity,
I stand dumb,
as in a holy place.

Same enamel pots for bread and toilet.
Piles of hair, gold fillings, prayer shawls,
massive piles of shoes
next to the metal doors into the showers.

At the end of obtuse silence, beyond the wall
stands the spiky Cross.
Carmelites bow low
to pray again our stupor.
"All we know is presence."

NELSON MANDELA

For twenty-seven years he built a house
of freedom within the house of pain.
Striking him, they scratched a match,
kindled a blaze beyond the prison bars
to set his lands aflame, put suns in lightless
midnight. The flashing sound of lash on his black
back nourished the razor of the nation's memory,
as his people bled to feed the soil the jailers trod.

For twenty-seven years he drew no syllogistic
judgment of revenge—blood for blood, grave
for grave—no clichéd homilies of cheap grace.
He breaks open truth's dungeon, uncages
robes of justice, erases the colored gavel,
un-apartheiding tables and toilets, unscrambling
the syntax of despair, un-poisoning the chalice,
drinking from the cup with those who locked his cell.
This is freedom. Here all can breathe.

SREBRENICA

The sky was clear that radiant day
Christian Slavs gunned the captives,
old men beside beardless boys in thousands
(distinctions never carry guns).
Moslem blood poured out like water.
No one notices the ground is red.

In retribution glorious, good measure,
pressed down, running over,
to pay in full, seventy times seven,
as Jesus said, four hundred years
of Moslem wrongs: fresh, raw.

At the last supper
Srebrenica eats her children.

One tongue in sister Slavic kin
under one Yahweh of the Covenant.
No matter. In a safe zone
Osman, Ali, Hasan, Hamza,
Slavs all: shot, buried.

The incense of hell fills
the sanctuary of masks
as the tractors genuflect
before the tabernacle of banality.

While the flesh is still upon the bone,
the earth newly dark and moist,
Hasans by the thousands are unearthed,
processed by machines for crushing ore,
consecrated with fire, anointed with lime,
baptized in industrial acid—a pasteurized
homogenized loam—bulldozed into a mine.

Guernica claws at the scab.
Out damn spot!

Who sees the Moslem dead twice killed,
twice shoveled under? Who weeps for Hasans
five hundred feet from sight?

The God of Abraham, Isaac, and Jacob sees.
The Yahweh of us all weeps over Srebrenica,
mourns the terror that will fall
like volcanic ash upon the Slavic lands
a thousand years.

COMING HOME IN KOSOVO

Across borders she slips, red
skirt in tatters, hunger in her face,
carrying a snotty child upon her hip
after weeks of bark and beetles for breakfast
in the hills. Sorrow died of starvation.

Even pain needs bread. Ten boy
soldiers, sullen with weariness of death,
pushed open the outside door she'd closed
against coming night, against
demons who straddle wars' hours.

Then she had been capable of fear,
the beginning of wisdom. They'd crowded
her kitchen. Her man still in the hay
field, expecting supper, coffee
steaming on the back burner turned

low, sliced ham on grandmother's
platter, half a loaf of raisin bread
crumbling on the side board. A rifle
shot across the currant patch.
August berries will not blood

his fingers. Death is not generic. The soldiers
quarreled over plums and jam in the pantry.
Captain, not twenty, leaning against
the balustrade, munching ham, wouldn't let
her bury her dead. Ten minutes to pack

her pain, lift two children and go.
Now back from the hills this hemlock day,
she moves among shards of glass,
torn baby blankets with giraffes,
marriage photos, he in a suit

too large, she in the family's white
lace—now grey—and mother's ivory
cameo, only yellow buttons
of her new blue dress. She toes the ashes
as women have done since it all began.

THE DAY OF THE CARDBOARD CUTTERS

8:45 a.m., September 11, 2001

Some who made it to the top
of our Himalayas perished there
when September was still young,
nonchalance still possible.

At the Guernica corner of Jerusalem/Nablus
confettied
ads of the dead.

Moslem martyrs reciting
Koran over strips of skin,
hands clinging to invoices,
welcomed to paradise by 72 virgins.

Ameritrade's Darwin:
Survival of the Fittest
Trade Simulator.

The electronic board flashing
galloping stock quotes,
savvy fiscal joy,
caught in the permanent present.

Beretta's 682 Gold:
Exclusive Shotgun
of the Year.

The heavens rain people.
Window on the World at the top,
dining for Lehman Brothers
turning soft dollars into hard money.

Marsh and McLennan offering
                            risk management
                                              insurance.

Our innocence lost
after the $15 martini
in the Greatest Bar on Earth,
a thurible of incense to Allah.

                              Nikko Securities
provides quality trade
          executions.

Rambo exports his decay
but clings to nonchalance: a stroll
in the park, the hand lolling
in the water behind the canoe.

The name of the Hercules Heavy
                            Recovery Tank is
                                      sur viv abil ity.

ELECTED MUSCLE AT MONASTIC MATINS

When the Lord your God gives them over to you and you defeat them, then you must utterly destroy them . . . and show them no mercy. Deuteronomy 7:2

Numbness is not yet *gravitas* as we rouse the dawn, spilling praises, yawns, and coughs around the white stone altar, dragging the bag of Israel's bones, reciting its warrior deeds, praying its defiant history.

With Moses we pass free through the Red Sea, smite Sihon, King of the Amorites, and Og, King of Bashan, who abides in Ashtaroth.

With Deborah we shout *Charge! The Lord has given Sisera into our hands.* With the strength of Yahweh's right arm we gather enemies to their fathers. *Happy shall he be who takes your little ones to dash their heads against a rock. Do thy wonders again in our day.*

We recognize election in its psalms: Yahweh will do transcendental violence, blood the hand to clear the land for Moses' people. No Dagan is nigh unto the Lord. Yahweh God generals Israel.

To the praise of God's glory we, too, are chosen, salt the Baghdad earth. We stop to fornicate with Baal in leafy groves of high places—warriors do these things—as we march for God, carrying the fury of Israel's psalmed past in our tanks, showing our elected muscle where it counts, singing "Praise to God who leads us!"

These iron chants we place upon the altar as our morning offering.

WHAT I SEE
FROM THE
BELL TOWER

IN PRAISE OF THE CLAY ANGEL

I thank you for the wonder of my being. Psalm 139:14

Gathered from the dust,
a little spittle

added for binding.
Given to itches,

pains in the head,
fallen arches,

flatulence.
Not promising, this

indecorous clod.
Still, a certain symmetry:

two eyes on different
sides of one nose,

the mouth mostly horizontal—
a wobbly monument to grace.

Before the clocks
began to measure movement

Yahweh spared a single breath
to give the mud some starch,

imparted a spasm
of his own life,

the disquiet of longing,
a reach to touch beyond,

gave it shards
of non-specific anguish.

A little less than angels,
an image of the One

who bent to breathe
upon it. I sing a new song

to the muck and wonder
of my being.

MY FAVORITE IDOL AND THE OTHER GOD

Come, let me show you my gilded god.
—I made it all myself—
It corrects the audit of my debris
with unforgiving eyes of emeralds,
sports an outsized ruby for an obscene
belly button, whose accusing rays
sign discontent with the incense I brought from Persia.
I enshrine this god-outside-myself, hanging it high
above a fake marbled mantel. From this purchase
it wardens all my prison twitches, twice
sifts my sins, computes my desertions.
As I snatch my joy in errant places
it hands down with rare dispatch, decrees
of reprobation etched in honest acid.

In a back alley of my choosing I met
a Separate Self my hands could not have formed,
who came in search by groping in my dark,
bumped against me as though by accident,
built a Sabbath rest in secret places,
an inner palace wherein to dwell, sup with me.
I was one of the mangy stragglers who let themselves
be found, where truth is mercifully adjusted.
To iniquity not blind, not deaf,
but slyly inattentive to lurches right,
stumblings left, less the walleyed judge,

more corruptible colluder.
Winces when it's called for, but compels
to banquet hall, noisy wedding dance,
supplying robes of glory for each beggar
to the scandal of the nine choirs of angels.

Count the bums between the seraphim.
Count, if you can. Who, friend, will believe you?

LILACS AND GALAXIES

Does he not leave the ninety-nine on the mountains and go in search of the one that went astray? Matthew 18:12

I was careless twenty, and upstart May
was shouting lilacs down the garden night.
I stopped along the cinder path to weigh
the choreography of stars and light,
wondered how God fingered galaxies,
laid down crisscrossed paths throughout the vault,
called by name black holes, fixed Pleiades,
relished endless light years to a fault,
gave the universe indecent space,
—which placed infinity in righteous doubt—
scattered dust so blindly it would disgrace
a drunken sailor strewing coins about.
  Between the blooming lilacs and the trees
  suddenly, kerplunk, I fell upon my knees.

I am careful eighty now and pick
my way along the cemetery path.
Perhaps, you'll say, I should be thinking thick
eternal thoughts to turn aside the wrath
of God from heaped-up sins. Not quite precise,
but smooth stupidities. Now there's the word:
stupidities; not sin, just dumb, the vice
of weary virtue at peace with the absurd.
The lilacs and the galaxies don't work

so well at eighty. Anyway, my knees
are shot; ecstatic plunking seems a pious quirk,
senility perhaps. Is dumb a boon to seize?
    The ninety nine are left for one dumb stray.
    Obtuse, inept, and dense: the surest way.

THE LADDER NOT CLIMBED,
THE BATTLE NOT FOUGHT

*Our struggle is not against enemies of blood and
flesh . . . but against cosmic powers of this present
darkness. Ephesians 6:12*

From the start I couldn't reach
the first rung of the long
ladder leaned against
the heavens, though I tried.

I cannot even see
the far end of the ladder
as though an enemy had hacked
off the head of an invader.

I'm not adept in battle against
demons with shield and sword.
Like David walking in Saul's
coat of armor, I cannot move.

But I'm fighting principalities
and powers in heavenly places
with an impertinent broomstick
and the courage of a hummingbird.

And there sits the god of my invention
like a weary Caesar at the Colosseum,
passive, willing to be appeased
on condition that I placate his anger

for my infamies, staying his sour
thumbs from slowly turning down,
opening up the lion gates
to certain public death.

Neither climb nor battle
is possible. I need some fool
to climb the ladder for me,
slay the upstarts in my stead.

GOD IS SILENT

Wait for the Lord and be strong. Psalm 27:14

Early I am up and doing,
brisk with wise resolve,

firm of purpose, pointed
as a letter of intent.

After years of muddled fidelity
they tell me I've got it wrong.

Be quiet and wait for Yahweh's
love. Let the Lord make

the first move and the last. So I've
shifted gears to apophatic heaths

and moors, where I wander in fake
inattention, wondering when the waters

move. Yahweh is surely
unreliable. I fall in my blood

at God's feet. No one raises me.
When I stand by the road, Yahweh

does not pass. When I open my mouth
to accuse, Yahweh refuses

to be summoned. Obviously, it is not
in the heavens to get crisp answers.

Yahweh uses tar and hemp
to calk the cracks. Without

the trench jargon, what's left?
Is silent darkness all I'll get?

JOHN BERRYMAN: *I DON'T THINK I WILL SING ANY MORE JUST NOW; OR EVER*

The steadfast love of the Lord never ceases, his mercies never come to an end. Lamentations 3:22

I've simply run out of hospitals.
No more adulterous *Sonnets* to Chris.
No more unmaking of marriage.
After I die there will be no more sin.

Six days a week I served Mass,
mumbling Latin prayers and piety,
stealing sips of altar wine,
the same two women rattling rosaries.

I stumbled through Columbia,
lurched down Princeton's avenues
in a whiskey sour: two parts groin,
one part God, and a jigger of ink.

Daemon transubstantiated
into demon, any bed would do,
ordered and disordered pain.
Vice is soluble in art.

A tipsy John the Baptist,
lifting a leg against the clods,
holding class in an uptown bar.
To hell with the administration.

Open wounds, but walking,
a detox louse, faithful
in my fashion: all I ever wanted
here was *Love & Fame.*

Like a repentant desert father
I give the word to my son:
Seek the Lord in silence.
You are loved even when you fail.

I can't say "I'm sorry" one more time.
I place my glasses on the sidewalk,
climb the railing of the bridge.
The Dream Songs have died.

MY UNCLE HENRY, THE LAWYER

Uncle Henry, a high-class ambulance-chaser, died suddenly.
The law on stilts—an eye for psychic buttons, checkered
vests, more masks than a Noh play—summations from
controlled rage to Homeric calm, gestures sprinkled with
speed-bumps, groped for chinks like Helen Keller feeling
the face of Annie Sullivan—opening a wee gap in the law
to tank maneuvers, slept with shot-glass in hand, law
abstracts for pillow.

Once his bear teeth grabbed your rump, he heard the
one-armed-bandit-rush of coins, scooping the cascade in
great tubs on the way to the cashier.

Devout in his statutory fashion, suffered Masses with
time off for good behavior, rosary in his desk, more Torah
than Moses, justification by faith messy— lacks forensic
precision— Protestants need the Code of Canon Law and
a no-nonsense Ratzinger pope.

Seventy percent of lawyers in the world live here. "The fear
of the Lord is the beginning of wisdom." Where lawyers,
there order. That's why casinos have poker guards with
cameras embedded in the ceiling, and lawyers waiting in
the wings for dirty business. Order, the breath of God,
is logic before Genesis, before God, founding member of
the bar, made Eve. Order triumphs as surely as a referee.
Every jot and tittle weighed and priced for storage against
the day the sun apocalypses into death.

Henry, seventy-five, ambulances faster, corridors full of children carrying brief cases, collapsed in court, died tort in hand, wondering about the order of his filing dates, if the wheels of the slot machine would stop at three cherries. And what about that poker guard peering from the ceiling, finger poised above the alarm?

I'VE COME TO SEE THE POPE

June 29, 1997

Up the Scala Regia,
   across the Court of Damascus,
through the painted threat
   of floggings, stonings, plagues
—all the sacred violence.

Above the gilded papal
   door a naked man
upon a cross nods mercy
   —unasked, unmerited, unmeasured—
to all who pass beneath.

Higher still a band
   of Raphael's empty virgins
with vapid veils march
   on the plaster grass
to offer plaster chastity.

On the brocaded wall Duccio's
   enthroned Lady Mary
presents her child,
   God's predatory Son.
An El Greco bleeds forgiveness

toward the crust of the indifferent.
   Swiss Guards in Medici stripes
of red and blue and yellow
   prod the sky with ersatz
halberds. Papal penguins

strut their starch before forbidden
   doors like domesticated seraphim
around the devouring fire.
   I've come to see the pope,
old man in white who mounts

Saint Peter's chair, a club-footed
   swan, wings heavy
with coffin smell, tidying up
   disorder in his nest, cuffing
subversive chicks. *The night*

light is on dim. Still, I see.
   Bellini, Bernini, Botticelli:
marble, lapis lazuli, ivory,
   pious booty of a dying prince,
do a princely prison make.

This thundering man, who drags
his cross toward the altar, does not falter.

A PLACE TO HIDE: LIGHT OFF

You are a hiding place for me. Psalm 32:7

Running on empty, I head for your palace,
shut the door on the cold. But no one

answers when I call your name. There's not
even a janitor's closet where I can

hunker down between dustpans
and industrial ammonia.
                              Of all your mansions,

none is more hung with damask and silence. So,
Lord, when you switch off

the one dangling light,
I grope around the moldy cellar.

I'll run on empty,
but I'm not going away.

A PLACE TO HIDE: LIGHT ON

You are a hiding place for me. Psalm 32:7

A fugitive looking for a cot
in your palace, I bring only

thirst, my self in buff,
and resolve. One can tell

a good hiding place by the way
the shelves are stocked:

Grand Cru Burgundy, olives,
mint, garlic, salt and manna.

You want only my poverty.
I offer the mess I've made

of my life. God, my refuge
forever, my new address.

MY FIRST HEARING AID

Must you mumble, garble
consonants, rush to the end,

drop last syllables?
Must I teach phonetics again?

Speak with precision. I am,
like Professor Henry

Higgins, a reasonable sort of man,
bearing malice toward none.

If only diphthongs were purer,
vowels and lives did not decay.

NOISES FROM
THE CLOISTER

LAUDS AND TROUBLE

My mouth is filled with your praise, and with your
glory all day long. Psalm 71:8

The rumpled brothers gather
to chant canticles across the choir
before the sun is up,

songs of printed gaiety,
rhapsodies of prescription joy.
Sun, moon, fruit

trees, birds on the wing
(. . . besides, it wasn't my turn . . .)
and all that moves in the waters

praise the Light that rises
like a bride's face peering
at the groom through lattices.

"Glory" the valley jungles
cry *(. . . If I were abbot! . . .).*
Only we are mute, must be taught.

In this moment of manufactured
ultimacy we hurl doxologies at God,
bow before the splendor

of darkness giving light
we cannot see, move
beyond the canned words

(. . . the cup was already cracked . . .),
to the throne, high and lifted up,
with the train of God's silence

filling the temple court,
the great hinges of the gates
groaning at the press of the Holy.

(. . . the Prior sings off key . . .). The Seraphim
bow, we hobble through Lauds,
steadfast in our small betrayals.

SAINT JOHN'S
TURKEY VULTURES

Forty Sherman tanks,
six foot wings,

red bullet-bald head,
battle-Cobra eyes,

soaring over dung-brown
barnyards, searching

for week-old afterbirths;
above I-94, spying out

road-kill cats
and death city.

Whatever stinks
they'll eat: dead rats,

dead fish, dead dogs.
Any Minnesota carrion.

Call the Abbot!
Toll the bell!

The buzzards circle
low above my cell.

IN SEARCH OF FIRE

Desire is the language of the soul. Gregory the Great

My knees are callused brown
from prayer; I'm as constant

as the hour bell, tolling
high upon the banner.

I pay my dues of praise
on time, four times a day,

twenty-six times a week
on black hardwood stalls,

(no velvet cushions for the monks).
I should be a teakwood torch;

instead I bring my rock
of ice for melting, carry back

the solid block. If desire's
the language of the soul,

my tongue's extinguished fire.
I pay my debts of praise

with frozen assets, but I pay.
Cold desire is still desire.

THIRST AND ROT
IN THE MONASTERY

Old sacks need much patching. Thomas Fuller

I'm old. My knees
buckle when I descend

the monastery stairs,
even when I grasp

the bark-brown banister
burnished smooth.

The vein in my right eye
burst some Hoover dam,

spilling globs of tired
blood to blur the not too

solid flesh. In the ears,
the precision miracle

of Siemens, sixteen
channels of sound,

full virtual reality.
What's most absurd,

arthritis in the right
thumb, pounding

jackhammer pain
so I keep vigils.

Decay and eighty-five,
like stink with cheese.

I've been seeking God
these many years,

thirsting for God's
presence like a hounded

deer panting
for water. But of late

I no longer thirst.
Sahara sands,

no desire for rain,
a sign of sin?

At the end the dying
shun food. Not wanting

water's the kind
of rot I can't abide.

KILIAN PARKS CAR C

As dark descends on St. Cloud
I go from door to door

with key, trying locks,
like a thief looking for loot,

down one row, up another,
searching for the car I think

I've parked beneath the purple elephant.
Or was it the checkered cow?

So many rows, so many animals.
When I am under the polka-dot pig

I turn around to find two oversize
policemen emerging from the dark.

Patting his holster, one asks
—*Just what do you think you're doing?*

—*Looking for my car. I forgot under
which animal I parked.—What make is it?*

—*I don't know. It's car C.*
—*Well, what color is it?*

—*I know it's not red, white and blue,
otherwise I don't know. It's car C.*

*—You mean you don't know either
  the make or the color.* The other officer,

Let me see your license. He reads
with his flashlight, turns the light

on me, an accused in a lineup.
Aha! The car thief's a monk from Saint John's.

IF I REACH EIGHTY-SIX . . .

The people stood at a distance, while Moses drew near to the thick darkness where God was. Exodus 20:21

Twenty-four, wanting
to profit God, I felt called

to the mound in the woods,
where absurd monks make

coffins in the barn, noises
in the church. Here I laid

my self upon the altar,
signed away my flesh to seek

the Holy One, who knows
but waits for my small coin.

Weak, beginning to be wise
at eighty-five I can no longer

work the pinewood planks,
or sing off key in choir.

Though spent, sleepy
in my choir stall, I can still

climb the mountain top
where God awaits my tip,

extended but still held fast.
I mount the dazzling darkness.

THE LAYING ON OF HANDS

Brother Hubert Schneider, o.s.b.,
1902–1995, carpenter

Certain things machines cannot do.
His Braille hands read
the close grain of the white oak.

He knows the woods by smell—
walnut: nutty; red oak:
acidic; plywood: formaldehyde.

Nothing wrong with knots,
like beauty spots upon the
cheek of a great queen.

He lays his hands on the cedar
plank like a bishop priesting
the palms of the deacon.

The resisting wood is wooed
into a "Yes, I do. I
plight my troth at the altar."

A prince in his horizontal forest,
like a Viking mingling his blood
with the Gauls, then vanishing.

That is my drawer.
Keeps his chisels sharp,
a surgeon ready to cut.

His tables chaste,
his chairs, true as the last
toll of the monastery bell.

It is not only the surface
of the wood, but I liberate
the praise chanting beneath.

When monks cheat at cards,
he stops. Nothing said.
When he wins, *I skunked him*.

I'LL DO IT TOMORROW

Godfrey Diekmann, O.S.B., 1908–2002

If you laugh, you flunk.
He backs into class,
face scratched,
fresh from a fall
on the ski slope.

Draws blood from drones,
speed from turtles,
even the snail
reaches the finish line
praising Irenaeus.

Twirling his glasses,
(half-scholar, half-ham)
writing left-handed,
his back to the blackboard:
Pray for Tertullian.

Only eternal life
is worthy of the name.
Not really rest,
but life supreme.
And we begin it now.

No bread on the altar,
no incense in the censer
unless the poor
have meat and bed.
The altar is in Selma.

Expert in liturgy
and lethal mushrooms.
No cluster of watercress
was safe, no chokecherry
unpicked in monk land.

Under his unmade bed
boxes of unopened mail:
uncashed checks,
unread manuscripts.
Purgatory here I come.

Every second leap year
(after pleas to reply)
he wrote a letter,
banging it out
on Wimmer's Underwood.

When he rose to speak
no one was his master:
insight, charm,
grand gestures, grand sighs.
We were all at his feet.

THE DEATH OF
MOUNT SAINT HELENA

Brother Frank Kacmarcik, Oblate, O.S.B.,
1920–2004

The room was full
when he sat alone,
like Mount Saint Helena
belching in the kitchen.

He knew he was anointed
above the others,
knew the oil
was not his own.

Infuriating critics
with papal decrees
from art's sole
Sedia gestatoria,

carried aloft
by twelve Swiss Guards,
Frank gesturing
to the commoners below.

No appeal for the visually
illiterate from less
is more; the holy
has the beak of a sparrow.

Enemy of the busy,
friend of visual silence,
he soared with the threat
of a condor looking for spleens,

ready to swoop
if you did not bow
before the sacred
meaning not uttered.

When his legs gangrened
beneath him, he allowed:
*I never fuss
what I cannot change.*

One March morning,
without a warning
burp, the volcano's
cone collapsed.

FRENCH VERBS, WHISKEY, HOLINESS

Emeric Lawrence, O.S.B., 1908–1999

Years moved like a reluctant glacier
as blind Emeric sat in the long darkness,
told his beads, spoke of little
Thérèse, tough lady, pawed

his way from chair to bed with the fatigue
of one ground down by tectonic ice;
shuffled down the corridor, stuttering
step, tentative, as though exploring

unexploded ordinance. On TV he heard
monks choiring praises in the church,
scraps of eternal Lauds snatched
from the quiet dark: the memory of God,

pharaohs, the wonders of the Red Sea,
some charismatic simpleton who embraced death
to set the captives free, take away
our prison rags, so that the last

lame beggar climbs the ladder
of delight. Gathered as a psalm those
endless days of teaching soft
French verbs to disobliging quarterbacks,

moving North Dakota jocks and Minnesota
lettermen from sin management, calculating
the distance to the border, making them seekers
of the Holy, *having no strange gods before me.*

A scribbler laying bare the wide intimacies
of God in many books, he mourned
the day he could no longer see
the blank unforgiving sheet. At six o'clock,

as if he expected a blazing visitation
from the court of heaven, he waited for the ungenerous,
too carefully measured nip. We carried
him up the high hill between the honor

guard of poplars, lowered him deep
in the primary soil, beside Martin,
Walter, Walbert, Dominic, and Baldwin,
among the great cloud of witnesses,

the grubby advanced guard, all breathing
eternal air, tarrying for that pokey
God, the apocalyptic palace coup,
moving bones in the resurrection thrill.

SUNDAY MORNING

Complacencies of prayer, and late shadows
scattering on the abbey's red brick,
a rush of light like a fistful of doubloons
cast down by a careless Arab prince
from the hush of the white baldachin,
wingspread of a great prehistoric falcon,
tinged with threat, lured to nest,
marking off the sacred where and why:
an acre of praise for a ton of glory.
Around the holy of holies the tarnished gather,
hesitating, torn between David's tears
and his dancing leaps before the ark moving toward Sion,
while green sidles through the windows into worship
as the spirea blooms white along the cloister walk
after the wide winter's last gasp.

The monks have come to the mountain of the Lord:
new ashes, old coals cover fire banked
a thousand years of seeking, sometimes
finding Who-Lives-in-Light-Inaccessible.
Everything can wait except the morning praise.
Black peacocks, crimson crows,
crippled sparrows, and one late robin,
in they file, compelled to come in
from the broadways and back alleys. By the book
they should be tormented by desire for the world

to come, tremble slightly for eternity,
but heavy of fork, deep of spoon,
they manage their tribute, stumble forward
toward the light where they see Light,
dim and fading, saying *Come.*

What a waste of manhood in these mutterings
in the night, making noises in the church,
these chaste chantings to empty spaces,
to an absent God who gives no answer,
whose paradise must wait, whose joy postponed
upon a promise made two thousand years ago
by some sweaty prophet who smells of fumble.
Why will not earth seem all of paradise
to them, that they must tarry here unwedded,
unbedded, untouched, unspent, and for what?
Is there only a rumor of blood in their veins,
making no passionate rounds, bleeding
soft pink when cut? Or do they bleed only
the blood of paradise that does not stain,
as they pluck the strings of insipid lutes?

Nothing has been lost, this Sunday morning,
no mountain stream left unattended,
no tree falls unnoticed, uncounted,
no pain not worth its solid weight,
no love not cherished, no regrets dismissed,

but they gather up the botched fragments left over:
the crust half eaten, a piece with the center
torn out, some slices cut too thin,
the burnt black top left on the sideboard,
one heel that fell upon the floor,
all collected into twelve massive
baskets placed upon the altar beneath the baldachin.
Divinity does not come only in shadows or in dreams,
but is hidden disheveled in the random fragments
that are not heaven, nor glory, but speak of them.

NOTES ON THE POEMS

Page 1. *"Ars scribendi / Ars moriendi."* The phrase *ars moriendi* (the art of dying) is a medieval monastic literary genre. Here it is combined with *ars scribendi* (the art of writing).

Page 4. "Eve and the Hermeneutic Task." Hermeneutics is the study of principles and interpretation.

Page 49. "Nelson Mandela." Composed in Harare, Zimbabwe, December 14, 1998.

Page 56. "Elected Muscle at Monastic Matins." *Charge! The Lord has given Sisera into our hands* (Judges 4:14); *Happy shall he be who takes your little ones to dash their heads against a rock* (Psalm 136:9). The passage from Deuteronomy 7:1-2 (to which one could add 20:16-18) is unsettling. The biblical text is presented as Yahweh's command to the Jewish people to commit genocide. Technically, this is called the ban (Hebrew: *herem*). Obviously, this evil practice cannot be a command of God. The Israelites were surrounded by countries which did indulge in this practice. It seems that the final editors of Deuteronomy in either the late exilic or early post-exilic period, centuries after the entry of the Jews into Palestine, took over this practice from their neighbors, and presented it as the will of Yahweh for the chosen people at the time of the Jewish occupation of the land. Further, scholars generally agree it is highly unlikely that, in actual fact, the ban was practiced in Israel either at the time of the entry into the land or later. That the command is found in an inspired text is problematic. However, this text, along with other vexing texts (e.g., death as punishment for adultery), must be situated in its historical context. The historical-critical method is decisive for determining the relevance of such texts for the twenty-first century. Unfortunately the problematic text has prompted some today to assume they are the military instruments of God's will.

The text from Deuteronomy is used here in the same ironic way Wilfred Owen used *Dulce et decorum est pro patria mori* (It is sweet and fitting to die for the fatherland).

Page 83. "In Search of Fire." Quotation from Gregory the Great, *Commentary on Job*, 2.7.11.

Page 84. "Thirst and Rot in the Monastery." Quotation from Thomas Fuller, *Gnomologia* (1732).

Page 92. "I'll Do It Tomorrow." Boniface Wimmer, o.s.b., of Metten Abbey in Bavaria was a pioneer Benedictine who in 1846 brought five students and fifteen brother candidates to found St. Vincent's Abbey in Latrobe, Pennsylvania. At the time of his death in 1887 he had founded five monasteries, including Saint John's Abbey.

Page 94. "The Death of Mount Saint Helena." The *sedia gestatoria* is a portable throne for the pope, carried by means of poles on the shoulders of the liveried Swiss Guards. It was used principally to bring the pope into the Basilica of St. Peter high enough above the congregation so the people could see him and receive his blessing. Because the *sedia gestatoria* is now seen as a relic of triumphalism, its use has been largely discontinued.

Page 98. "Sunday Morning." After Wallace Stevens' "Sunday Morning."

A POET IN THE MONASTERY:
I DO NOT TELL "NOBLE LIES"

Years before he was elected Benedict XVI, Cardinal
Joseph Ratzinger said that at the end of the day there are
only two arguments for Christianity: the saints in the
church, and the art that grows in her womb. The saints let
the experience of God's holiness transform them.

One could ask whether religious experience is translat-
able. If translation means enclosing the infinite in the finite,
yes, it is untranslatable. But we experience the shadows of
God's holiness reflected on the wall of the cave. And the
holiness of God echoes through its vastness. The shadows
and echoes we experience we can translate. This is not
the direct and immediate experience of God, as religious
extravagance sometimes suggests. Such language is mere
rhetoric. No one attains face-to-face immediacy this side
of death. When theologians try to capture religious expe-
rience in words they resort to the clumsy, contradictory
language of "mediated immediacy" (Heribert Mühlen).
No unmediated experience of God's holiness exists. Always
something separates God and the experience of God. In
this betweenness stand art and poetry. "The poet names
the holy," says Martin Heidegger.

Back in the eighteenth century Samuel Johnson hedged
on even the possibility of religious experience being the
basis for poetry. Poetry is about intensity. That is, religious

poetry reaches for something transcendentally higher than itself in order to capture it and bring it down into the poem in intensified form. But God is so exalted, so far removed, Johnson recalled, that poetry does not have the capacity to confer intensity of this kind. Theology is "too simple for fiction, too majestick for ornament," he wrote. Further, the essence of poetry is surprise. What little is known of God has already been said. There can be no surprises in religious writing and, Johnson concluded, religious poetry is always hopelessly lame.

Strangely enough, surprise is the second name for the word of God, for instance, the eruptions of God in history there recorded. These interventions are recorded in the psalms and biblical narrative texts of monastic prayer. When summing up the meaning of monastic life Saint Benedict asks, "What page, what passages of the inspired books of the Old and New Testaments are not the truest guides for human life?" And I would add, for the monastic poet. The poet in the monastery has this in common with the beginnings of American poetry, indeed, the beginning of modern poetry. In an essay entitled "The Bible as Poetry," Walt Whitman tells of going to the seashores of Long Island for a week at a time, lolling on the beach to read, among other things, the Old and New Testaments. He declared that the books of the bible "are the fountainhead of song." Indeed, scriptural themes play a major role in his later poetry.

Monastic life was built on the poetry, poetic narrative, and poetic imagination of the scriptures. The monks of Saint Benedict's time in the sixth century learned by heart the whole of the Psalter, 150 psalms. These were recited antiphonally by heart in choir. When they came together for the office of Vigils the community listened to one of the monks read from the Old and New Testaments. While at work in the shops and fields they masticated the biblical texts they had memorized, chewed on them as a cow chews the cud of food already eaten. Also they spent long hours each day in *lectio divina* (divine reading), most frequently the scriptures. *Lectio divina* is a kind of prayer, a slow reading of God's word with the heart.

When I entered the monastery in 1945 I inherited a modified form of this tradition, almost sixteen hundred years of lived experience of the biblical/liturgical/classical culture, expressed within in the context of common prayer and common meals. Twenty-six times a week the monks of Saint John's Abbey come together to pray the psalms or to celebrate the Eucharist. In addition we pray the text of scripture in private. Monastic poets agree with Whitman, the scriptures are truly the "fountainhead of song."

Besides the scriptures I also have daily contact with the sacramental life of the church, especially the Eucharist. In the sacramental mode one is invited to share the interior reality that physical matter (bread, wine, water) signs (points to) and symbolizes (makes present) through the proclamation of the word. The sacramental mode makes it possible to catch voices that make no sound in the air. As the Son of God is made visible and accessible in the flesh of Jesus Christ, in a similar way the weight and force of God's presence is accessible through the materiality of oil, water, wine, and bread. Both scripture and sacrament invite the monk to doxology. We kneel in praise of God's glory dwelling beyond space and time, but active in our bumbling space, in our crippled time. Without violating its own inherent discipline, religious poetry is one great doxology to the praise of God's glory. To paraphrase the second-century theologian Irenaeus, I want my poetry to be in accord with the Eucharist and for the Eucharist to confirm it. Both scripture and the Eucharist draw the monk into solitude.

Monks "leave the world" to seek God and the glory of God. The Unitarian soul of Ralph Waldo Emerson was not thinking of monasticism when he encouraged the poet to "leave the world." Emerson sounds like a reforming Benedictine abbot when he writes that poets should avoid "the times, customs, graces, politics or opinions of men." One need not enter a monastery to leave the world in Emerson's sense. Only draw in and back. Originality, the ability to say a new thing, comes out of this retreat. The monk/poet will bring forth a host of new images and possibly a new language if he truly seeks God and God's glory in silence within the biblical/liturgical culture of the monastery.

If one finds newness one will not fall into "sameness," producing what Donald Hall calls the "McPoem, the same from coast to coast . . . ten billion served." These hamburger poems are subject to the quality control of the least common denominator. One of the ways of escaping sameness is to feed on a different kind of bread. I am not suggesting that the biblical/liturgical culture of Catholicism has never been tapped before. Obviously, that is not true. But Robert Lowell recognized new possibilities in its riches, saying that the principal reason for his conversion to Catholicism was its rich symbolic life, as Dr. Martha Meek remarked. The Bread of Life found in the great Catholic tradition is new for millions (including Catholics), and will feed thousands of poems, with twelve baskets of surprises left over. Dante, who is one of my anchors in the tradition, demonstrates that the tradition is ever fertile, giving the poet new things to say.

Does a poet need something to say? Or can the poet simply dazzle with images, the beauty of language? Elizabeth Barrett Browning detected in John Keats "the want of thought as thought." In a word, he had nothing to say. Siegfried Sassoon once asked the question, "What shall the minstrel sing?" His conclusion: he had nothing to sing about, apart from his war experiences. The poet cannot simply trot out the old lilacs and daffodils, though nature poetry has an affinity to monastic life, which is generally agrarian. Poetry should not teach, but can it be pure intensity? Can it have something to say? For me the poetic truth is somewhere between William Carlos Williams' "No ideas, but in things," and Jack Spicer's "The truth is that pure poetry bores everybody. It is even a bore to the poet." Between those extremities my monastic life provides me with unheard of songs. "O sing the Lord a new song" (Psalm 98:1).

How high can the monk/poet aspire? What about ambition? Saint Paul counsels "do nothing out of selfish ambition or vain glory" (Phil 2:3). In chapter seven of *Rule for Monks,* the longest of the seventy-three chapters, Saint Benedict speaks of the twelve steps on the ladder of humility. How does a monk/poet reconcile mounting this ladder with poetic ambition? Gerard Manley Hopkins solved the problem one way. By the time he entered the Society of Jesus he already had written a hundred poems. Before leaving for the novitiate he burned some of them, a symbolic massacre of the innocents, indicating that he had given up one vocation for another. I protest. The two vocations are perfectly compatible. After delivering his conferences to his monks on the highly sensual Song of Songs, Abbot Bernard of Clairvaux went back to his cell to polish the language in view of publication. Not an exercise in lamentable pride. When you sing to God's glory, you aim high.

Does aiming high mean writing poems, but not publishing them? Some religious poets published either few or none of their poems, among them George Herbert, Andrew Marvell, Hopkins. Possibly Emily Dickinson belongs on the list. Hopkins had his friend Robert Bridges as his literary executor, a friend who was in no hurry. Thirty years after Hopkins' death Bridges published Hopkins' poems, and then with denigrating comments.

The religious poet does not write simply to get published. Ostensibly he writes to communicate and that would ordinarily include publication. The poets named above did not want their poetry to perish with them. Religious consecration does not mean the absence of religious ambition. Where is the locus of ambition? Hall limits ambition to the poet. I extend it also to the poem. Williams' "The Red Wheelbarrow," a poem of eight lines totaling sixteen words, is not as ambitious as *Paterson*, a book of 236 pages. The ambition is not in length, but in what Williams attempts.

More often than not the poet has too little ambition rather than too much. Hall suggests that if one does not have the ambition to write poems as great as Dante, why write at all. Why clutter the world, he asks, with "McPoems"? Though I don't write poetry in order to become famous, I aspire to kindle a pillar of fire that will last. Otherwise, it's a waste of time. However, I've never been successful, and almost certainly, never will be. I still write bad poems, mediocre poems. I'm an amateur at eighty-five. James Dickey argued, "Every writer is a failed writer. We're all amateurs at this. We don't live long enough to be anything else." Nonetheless, I aspire.

And to help me along the way I have four prize-winning poets as mentors. Michael Dennis Browne, my teacher in Iowa City, critiqued and edited my *Swift, Lord, You Are Not*. Dr. Martha Meek, the editor of *Yahweh's Other Shoe*, not only close-read many drafts of my poems, she repeatedly drove eighty miles to the monastery to discuss my poetry with me. Jay Meek, a nationally recognized poet, made appropriate noises from the background. Daughter Anna George Meek critiqued my Prodigal Son poems. It's a family affair. With such mentors I have to be ambitious, especially because, having started to write poetry in a serious way at seventy-five, at eighty-five I have limited time to develop.

This is not religious pride. Hall has expressed the literary reasons for high ambition. To these I add biblical reasons. The books of Leviticus and Numbers record over forty times that Yahweh commanded the Israelites to make a sacrifice of a bull, ram, or ewe "without blemish." "You shall offer an animal without blemish before the Lord" (Lev 3:1). The Israelites were not to place on the altar of sacrifice a sick animal that was going to die within the week anyway. No, they were to offer the best they had. I want to place my best on the altar of praise.

If I strain at ambition, the poem will betray it. Nonetheless, I still want each poem to be ambitious for itself, though not in the grand style. I could not write poetry with the architectural complexities of Pindar or the lush bravura of Dylan Thomas. Rather I want my poetry to have the simplicity and depth akin to consecrated bread and wine. The hard-edged simplicity of this kind brings its own elegance and power. Patrick Kavanagh noted that poetic simplicity "is the ultimate in sophistication." Simplicity may also mean publishing less. Eliot published little. In a writing career that spanned fifty years Elizabeth Bishop published only about ninety poems, averaging less than two a year.

The ambitious struggle for simplicity is related to the question of meaning. Socrates complained that poets of his day could not explain the meaning of their words. When asked the meaning of a poem she had written, Marianne Moore answered, "I knew when I wrote it." Wallace Stevens did not always know what his poetry meant. Simplicity in my vocabulary does not mean that everything is immediately transparent, or that my words have only surface meaning. If I am inviting the reader to experience with me the mystery of God, then the clarity is not that of a tractor manual. I do not mind challenging the reader, and I want the reader to come back later, read my poem again.

Does the ambition of my poems extend to changing people's lives? One editor of my poetry suggested I was giving religious lectures, aimed at transforming lives. Not really. When W. H. Auden wrote "poetry makes nothing happen" he was taking sides in the debate started by the ancient Greeks concerning the aesthetic and social responsibilities of art. The pre-Socratic Greek poets put poetry at the service of morality. In his own way Plato followed them. Though he was a poet by nature, he barred poets from the ideal republic. Plato thought poets told "noble lies" (before him Pindar termed them "glorious lies"). Poets were, therefore, not civically responsible. If, however, poets promoted morality, the door to the ideal republic was open. The function of poetry, Plato said, is to teach. The old Puritan distrusted poets because they appealed not to reason, but to the passions. But he cheated. After his death a book of poetry was found at his bedside.

Plato's student, Aristotle, seems to contradict his master by saying the function of poetry is to give delight. But Aristotle has a more nuanced view. For him learning is the greatest delight. The good poet delights by his special manner of imparting knowledge. William Wordsworth contended that "every great poet is a teacher," and added, "I wish either to be understood as a teacher, or as nothing." Percy Shelley thought poets were "the unacknowledged legislators of the world" (which he cribbed from Johnson). Robert Frost's poetry is highly didactic; Ezra Pound thought one was speaking "rubbish" if one said that art should not teach; Auden moved from an isolated lyricism to the didactic when his "September 1, 1939" promoted antineutrality in Europe; Stevens implies the boundaries of temporal life contain all there is: "Shall our blood fail? / . . . And shall the earth seem all of paradise that we shall know?" (a view he later renounced). Eliot's "The Love Song of J. Alfred Prufrock" indicts an effete society.

I could use these greats as my models, but I don't. I recognize the peril in subordinating poetry to extra-poetic ends, even to religious ends. In China and the Soviet Union art and poetry were reduced to stagnation by being ordered to serve the state. Perhaps even Girolamo Fracastoro (1483–1553) goes too far when he wrote, *"in a measure* teaching is the concern of the poet, but *not* his peculiar capacity." Unlike Wordsworth, I do not want to be a teacher. My poems are not spiritual conferences. My basic paradigm in writing religious poetry is Jacob wrestling with God, confronting God, as in my poem "God Cheats." I wrestle with God "flesh to flesh, sweat to mystery" and I limp away. I invite the reader to stand close enough to smell the sweat, hear the heavy breathing, enter the mystery, experience what I experience as I challenge God on the mat. I invite the reader to limp away with me.

I have written a poem, not included in this book, entitled "Mary Magdalene: Banned by Law," which could be interpreted as a lecture on women's rights. I contend it is not. In the poem Christ chooses the steady Mary Magdalene to be the first witness of the resurrection rather than the unsteady Peter. Because the Magdalene was a woman and thought to be unreliable, she was not allowed by law to witness in court. But the testimony of the unsteady Peter could be accepted. Still Christ challenges social roles, sending the Magdalene to witness to Peter on the central truth of his message. If I impart a truth when I relate my experience of the Magdalene and Peter texts, it is, as Michael Schmidt wrote, "in the truth of the telling." I am not teaching but sharing an experience; truth tags along.

Sharing experience lies close to my personal life. An editor encouraged me to write more about my personal life as a monk. I am ambivalent. This means moving towards the "I" in poetry. The use of the "I" as the personal self did not start in the twentieth century. You can find it in the early Greek poets, Hesiod (8th *c.* B.C.E.), Archilochus (8th *c.* B.C.E.), Alcman (7th *c.* B.C.E.), and Sappho (7th *c.* B.C.E.).

The "I" of early Greek poets has a more open subjectivity than that of twentieth-century confessional poets. The "I" of the Greeks is a lyric "I," personal in character, but reflecting a common experience. I can identify my experience with that expressed in the early Greek poetry. The "I" was enhanced because the poem was recited to music composed by the poet, accompanied by an instrument, often the lyre, played by the poet. Music and poetry have a common birthday; only later were they divorced.

Another group of poets, those who write personal poems, technically called "confessional" poetry, use the "I" in a quite different way. Confessionalism is the name twentieth-century literary critics gave to the poetry of Robert Lowell, Sylvia Plath, Anne Sexton, W. D. Snodgrass, and John Berryman. Here the "I" is more enclosed, more the public exposure of private pain, sometimes extremely private, as when Lowell wrote poems quoting, without authorization, the private letters of his wife referring to their troubled relationship. "Don't you dare mail us the love your life denies; do you really know what you have done?" The judgment of the critics was that this is merely personal, idiosyncratic, and without societal or universal meaning. Hall mercilessly called it "narcissistic self-exploitation." Hall himself wrote the moving *Without* about the death of his wife/poet Jane Kenyon. But his approach is not confessional, but personal, reflecting universal experience of husbands who have lost their wives. *Without* does not express only private pain. The line between personal and confessional is thin, but real.

The thinness of the line causes my ambivalence. Crossing the line has monastic implications. Who do I think I am, to parade my private pain as though it were socially significant? I do not want to be identified with the stance of the Beat poet, Gregory Corso: "I am the substance of my poetry." For a monk that would be a radical dislocation. I understand why early the very term "confessional" became a pejorative label, resented by some. Nonetheless, I recognize that for the poet to be close to the experience of the clearly defined speaker in a poem, the "I," presents opportunities. To write from intimacy can give immediacy, and moves the poet away from the abstract, the objective to the concrete. I have written some deeply personal poetry, for instance, "A Place to Hide: Light Off" and "A Place to Hide: Light On" about my experience of the frustration and joy in prayer. These poems I do not consider "narcissistic self-exploitation," or "confessional." This experience I share with everyone, including non-monastics, who take the quest for God seriously and make prayer part of the rhythm of the day.

My concern is less about my poetry being confessional and more about talent. Do I really have the gift? Am I just another scribbler manufacturing inspirational verses for Hallmark greeting cards? Like all artists and poets, I live and sleep with doubt. Eliot is my comfort: "No intelligent writer knows if he is any good." But what do all the rejection slips mean? The poet needs affirmation and cannot live on unmitigated failure. A monastery is not a domicile for poets. Still the symbolic ethos, the communal liturgies, Scripture, silence, private prayer, and the support of brothers suggest that if a poet cannot thrive here, then nowhere.

I get considerable support from my brother monks. After hearing me read three poems at a meeting, Abbot

John Klassen, and university president Brother Dietrich Reinhart, o.s.b., suggested that Saint John's University Press publish my poems. As a result *Swift, Lord, You Are Not* appeared in 2003. At Christmas the Abbot and President promoted my book by giving it as a present to friends.

Monasteries, however, are reflections of society. Only about five percent of the public read poetry, and many, indeed very many, cultured persons will not go across the street for a poetry reading. A major poet/critic like Hall once gave a reading at Saint John's University. Only about thirty persons showed up, four of them monks. Another example: Some years ago a talented young monk artist was sent out for professional training in sculpture. On a cold blustery February evening after he returned from study he gave a lecture and exhibited some of his sculptures in the Art Building, which is on the edge of the campus, some three hundred feet from the monastery. About the same time I gave a poetry reading, literally a few feet down the warm corridor from the monastery. I remember three monks attending. I am not less loved; poetry is not of general interest.

But then there is the great liturgist, Father Godfrey Diekmann, o.s.b. Godfrey was my professor in the 1940s. He was the master, I the disciple. Even in my eighties I never graduated. Shortly before Godfrey died he was flat on his back in the monastic infirmary, gasping for breath through an oxygen tube, the stainless steel side-guards locked in place. As though speaking to me on the way out the door, he said, "Kilian, stop writing theology! Write poetry! You are good at poetry."